PEECHES
& KREEME

Gotham Books

30 N Gould St.
Ste. 20820, Sheridan, WY 82801
https://gothambooksinc.com/

Phone: 1 (307) 464-7800

© 2024 *Deon Llewellyn*. All rights reserved.

No part of this book may be reproduced, stored in a retrieval system, or transmitted by any means without the written permission of the author.

Published by Gotham Books (July 13, 2024)

ISBN: 979-8-3303-3857-3 (P)
ISBN: 979-8-3303-3858-0 (E)

Because of the dynamic nature of the Internet, any web addresses or links contained in this book may have changed since publication and may no longer be valid.

The views expressed in this work are solely those of the author and do not necessarily reflect the views of the publisher, and the publisher hereby disclaims any responsibility for them

TABLE OF CONTENTS

Acknowledgement vi

Do Not Forget 2

Children 3

True Friends 4

Birthdays 5

For My Son 6

For My Children 7

Life 8

O My God 9

O M G 10

Stress 11

Entitlement 12

It's About Me 13

Laundry Day 14

Sunny Day 15

Education 16

Street Smart 17

Confidence 18

Culture 19

Jamaica 20

Grand Child 21

Parents 22

Vacation Time Staycation Time 23

God	24
Inheritance	25
Only Child	26
Respect	27
Employment	28
Lonely Heart	29
Pets	30
Father	31
Back Up Plan	32
Single Dad	33
Future	34
Mother	35
Survival	36
The Moon Has A Rainbow	37
Forever	38
Let It Go	39
Storm	40
Love Recipe	41
Author Bio	42

ACKNOWLEDGEMENT

Dedicating this book to my parents.

Leonard and Evelyn Llewellyn who have always showed me love affection and believing in myself.

My son Corey Llewellyn who has kept me focus and fill my heart with joy.

To all my friends especially Grace Jenkins who always insist I should be a writer and encouraged me to fulfill my writing dream.

Special thanks and gratitude to Shelwyn Hendy who has supported and encouraged all my ideas and accomplishments, goals, and dreams.

To the special people in my life.

PEECHES
& KREEME

Deon Llewellyn

Do Not Forget

Roses are red violets are blue.
I don't want flowers I only want you.
You are my make up kit;
My purple lipstick.
Don't worry about it
Our lips are meant to kiss.

Children

We went and got them.
They did not ask to come
unfortunately they are dumb.

Don't lose yourself.
Don't lose your mind.
You will end up in jail getting grind.

Enjoy yourself.
Enjoy your life.
God gave it to you.
Don't lose it due to anger.

True Friends

Love is being patience.
Patience gets you everywhere without fear.
You have true friends.

Fear makes you miss your future and your today.
It makes your tomorrow but your true friends will stay.

Remember there is no tomorrow,
only today make the best of it.
Yesterday is gone and tomorrow never comes.
The true friends you have will be there for the show down.

Today will always be here.
True friends know who you are.
Do you know who your true friends are.

Birthdays

Birthdays are special because you are blessed.
Birthdays are special because you are the best.
Loving soda and upgrade to juice shows that
with birthdays comes maturity.

Faith in life lets you enjoy each day in harmony.
Blessing love and faith starts the new
celebration of life all over again.

For My Son

When the sun comes up Corey is bright.
It lets me know he will be alright.

My son has his ways it makes me wonder
how he sees life is it a ponder.

Corey will never tell on you.
I guess he prefers to be amused.

He has matured and grown nicely
well-mannered and secure.

Corey will be Corey that's for sure.

For My Children

When the sun comes up my children are bright.
It makes me know they will be alright.

My children have their ways it makes me wonder.
How they see life is it a ponder.

My children will never bully or tell on you.
I guess they prefer to be amused.

My children have matured and grown nicely
well-mannered and secure.

My children will be my children that's for sure.

Life

Enjoy what you have and what is to come.
Life is beautiful in all situations
you may go through.

It is the best thing to know.
Life offers what one needs to grow.
Never think twice always choose life.

O my God

OMG he ask me.
OMG he give me the ring.
OMG he says its only me and him.
OMG I love him.
OMG she say yes.

OMG I am going to give her the best.
OMG I deserve her.
OMG we love each other bad.
OMG we started as friends.
OMG we can't pretend.

OMG we are going to the church.
OMG we are going to be each other's night nurse.
OMG, OMG, OMG.
Yes, it will always be.
OMG, OMG, OMG.
him and me.

OMG

OMG im hask mi
OMG im gi mi de ring
OMG im say a only mi an im
OMG mi love im

OMG she say yes.
OMG mi a go giv er de bess
OMG mi deserve er
OMG mi love er bad

OMG wese wan a neda like Fren
OMG we caan preten
OMG we a go a de church.
OMG we a go be wan a neda nite nurse

OMG, OMG, OMG it will always be
OMG, OMG, OMG im an mi

Stress

S - Sweet as honey nice as candy.

T - Trust in everything you do, don't let anything disappoint you.

R - Remember everyone will be wrong but your patience keeps you going strong.

E - Every day is beautiful pain, negativity, sadness and failure should encourage smile laughter and perseverance.

S - Sentimental feelings thoughts and fulfillment make the mind great.

S - Stay calm don't be alarm don't stress.

Entitlement

Don't tell me I am entitled to it because I will utilize it.
Let me know my entitlement so I will not lose it.
Entitlement is a noun.

Claim the entitlement to all that is presented.
Let it be known there are ways to fulfill them with enjoyment.
Entitlement is a verb.

Yes, entitlement is great it lets you appreciate.
What you are to receive but do not over abuse it.
Entitlement is a word that can be used however you choose.
Make sure to utilize it don't jeopardize it.
Entitlement is an adjective.

It's About Me

My parents love me this I know.
It's about me because they tell me so.

My life is beautiful this I know,
because I smile always and it helps me grow.

It's about me I know.
I love me and I let it show.

It's about me; I know my family lets me know.
It's about me this I know.
I feel it in my heart and my soul.

Laundry Day

Wash, wash, wash all my clothes away,
No, No, No let me iron every day.
Laundry day is boring time consuming.
Yes, clothes have to be clean but for me ironing is everything.

Laundry day is important that we know,
but the exotic aroma of the iron on the clothes
clears your sinus and open up your nose.

Laundry day is great,
but not everyone wants to participate.
I hope to find someone who loves it.
Give me the iron and you will know.

That my best is going to be in everything that I press.

Sunny Day

Days are ways to know and judge how we feel.
Days always make it great overall no big deal.

Snowy day, play day, rainy day and cloudy day.
Yes, there are many days but the best is Sunny day.

Money day, poor day, emotional day, mental health day
but the best day is sunny day.

There are 8 days in the week.
Sunday, Monday, Tuesday, Wednesday,
Thursday, Friday, Saturday.
The best and 8th day, is sunny day.

As you can see the week starts on Sunday,
and end on the best Sunny day.
It's the day that makes you feel the best.

Family Day, Friend Day, Couples Day, People Day, Every day,
but we all have to have Sunny days.

Education

To learn is to understand.
It cannot be taken away, Education.
To grow is to know.
that knowledge we will always have.
Education will be the number one,
without it there is no progression.

Education is not an inheritance.
It is a seed we have to plant.
Nurture your education watch it grow and mature.
It now becomes your future and opens the doors.
Don't wonder what to do make sure and educate you.

Life is the best without any impression,
but education gets you out of oppression.
We must move on and be strong.
The lack of education can cause us to lose,
our opportunity and our ambitions.

Education is the key
but the foundation needs to be there
so educate yourself it will only be fair.
It cannot be taken away.
Education is the high way.

Street Smart

We can be right or wrong
but common knowledge is our bond.
Street smart is about your hopes and dreams.
Street smart can never be seen.
Get the flow of it let it go never figure it out.
It definitely has no doubt.

Street smart is how you use it;
Never underestimate it.
It is intense it is hard but street smart makes you go far.
Think it through know what to do.
Never dismiss it you will always need it.
Oh, how it works street smart will teach it all

It is true you will survive let it be you.
Yes, it gives you preview.
It is smooth, it is cool, it makes you feel brand new.
Street smart is wise so to use it we will all survive
It is risky not always good
but remember it can be used by everyone.

Never forget we are all street smart.
There is no DNA, XY chromosome no blood type
no stereotype.
It is well known we all are street smart bond.

Confidence

It's a big word that can be confused.
It's the word we have to embrace.
It's the word that's in our motto.
Confidence I got you.

Confidence sweet calm and relaxing.
The feeling gives you all you need
and can make you over achieve.
This feeling has behavior that works in any favor.
We learn it but we have to implement it.
If we don't, we should not use it.

Confidence is like a butterfly and you will know why.
It goes from a caterpillar to a cocoon,
a hard storage home that produces a butterfly.
Confidence revealed and you will see why,
from a worm to a – beautiful butterfly.

Confidence and you ask why.
It shows there are no alibies.
Never give up just remember,
Confidence gets you through
from January to December.

Culture

Where did it come from the meaning of culture.
Is it created by ideas or feelings.
Is it important or a thing never to be revealed.

A child with no knowledge will guess at everything
but the meaning of culture they learn many things.
Who what why how when; the meaning of culture will have no end.
So here is culture no matter where or why it helps to diversify

Culture is how you speak, eat, socialize, entertain and organize.
Culture is the manners you learn.
It is the door to the attic the basement and the front door.
It also elevates you to higher floors.

Culture is how you dress not to impress but perform your best.
It's the food, the beliefs, the security, the story.
Culture can give you glory.
It is Pre-K to First grade, it goes on to higher grades.

Culture makes up the education scale.
Take it with you
know what it is and what it means.
Culture is an enhancing cream.

Jamaica

How can you say you discovered it we were not lost.
How can you claim it when we already made it.
How can you! Control it when we know how to mold it.
JAMAICA

Wood and water we have it.
Rivers and beaches, it completes us.
Mountains, hills, and waterfalls is our know-it-all.
Herbs and plants we grow them.
We also know how to utilize them.
Hibiscus flowers, Ackee and Salt fish
our horticulture and national dish.
The Humming Bird our motto
let you know we got you.
Meditation. Relaxation.
JAMAICA

We are of descendants, migrant, indentured servants
out of many one people.
Professionals trade people, street people market people,
entrepreneurs are known by everyone,
and they all understand.
JAMAICA

We little but we talawa
spicy and nice ready to fight.
We always choose to unite
Diverse in culture language tourism adventure
food and rhythm.
We know to always be wrong, and strong
but we are also west Indian-best, in the Caribbean.
Best of all and important don't forget we are.
JAMAICANS

Grand Child

Mother father sister brother
no one is the best but the grandchild.
The smile the cry the beady eyes
it looks the best on the grandchild.
The chubby cheeks the cute button nose
the first tooth lets you know
the grand child is here to grow.

The tiny fingers, the tiny toes
and the tiny earlobes.
The smile, the bright eyes,
the give-me-what-I-want when I cry.
Yes, that is the grandchild.
Love them, they represent you
let them know how to be true.

It's your grandchild.
They are beautiful, they are great,
they are here to let you celebrate.
Yes, the grandchild.

We love them we adore them
we comfort, and discipline them.
Train them to be good to themselves.
We also have to listen,
learn from them.
They will always be the grandchild.
Thank God for mothers, fathers,
sisters, and brothers
but most of all the grandchild.

Parents

To have fun to love teach and nurture.
We understand and give a helping hand.
We show the way we communicate.
Parents let it be known we will never leave you alone.
We can nag we can be mad.
We will disagree and get them sad.
We let the children be themselves.

We hold them mold them as parents.
We console them.
We have a duty and responsibility
because we want to communicate with unity.
Parents are fun and great.
We give them everything to celebrate.
We spoil them and adore them.
Most of all we let our children know it's about them.

Parents adapt parents set traps.
We encourage and fill in the gap.
We are strong and have to get along.
Parents try to show their success.
We are stern and always concerned.
Like water 'under the bridge,
we instill all that is positive.
Life gives us lessons we have to teach.
It lets us know not to always preach.
Parents we are without a doubt.
Hip, Hip Hurray
Parents knows and show the way.

Vacation Time
Staycation Time

Stay home go away go near go far
take time make time vacation
or you can call it staycation time.
Have fun enjoy life don't say not to day.
Waiting to retire and say it is vacation time
will become why didn't I take the time.
We cannot put off fun when it comes.
Never wait always navigate and appreciate
vacation or staycation time.
Have a great vacation time staycation time.
It's great to explore
go out the door
to enjoy vacation or staycation time.

Money is great
we need it to participate
but remember vacation staycation should not wait
Our body and mind know vacation and staycation time.
Listen keenly to the water fall, the waves on the beach,
the food the music, the scenic route, the ski,
mountain climbing, bicycle ride,
the walk through the park.
Vacation time staycation time it's fun
Just take it anytime.

God

Let us recognize who he is.
We were molded by him because that was his decision.
He has our perfect water in his reservoir.
Nothing but sunshine and the best his name is God.

Never lose yourself in anyone else.
Listen with your eyes, see with your ears,
taste with your nose, and smell with your tongue,
Walk with your hands, and touch with your feet.

We trust in him and reversing these things;
he shows us to believe in him.

His name is God.

Inheritance.

What can we say about it.
Do we deserve it or should it be an obligation.
Inheritance is it a lazy way for us to be complete.

It comes from love ones but do we deserve it.
Inheritance has been around since the beginning of time
but is it our only survival line.

Oh, how glorious for inheritance but do we deserve it.
The giver has prepared for us but do we deserve it.
Do good and expand with it but do we deserve it.

Is it a tradition or is it an obligation.
A let me show my love and appreciation.
Inheritance do we deserve it.

Let us ask inheritance the question direct
Should we wait and see is that for me
Should we feel it is our right to get what we seek

Should we hold our breath and say:
let me get or should we look into ourselves and say hey
inheritance are you the only way
We should all prepare for our own
don't consider to get it not as a loan
We should know we get what we reap
not always what we sow.

Remember we are always looking for it but heck
the inheritance we receive do we deserve it.

Only Child

oh boy oh boy it's only me
oh boy oh boy this I see
Yes, yes I will never fall
Yes, yes I get it all

spoiled I am you do understand
but not to the point where my parents wont
raise their hands and let me know who is in command.

Only child it is sweet but sometimes it
would be nice to have siblings to make you
feel complete.

Only child that I am see
how life grows with parents that understand
and help with all your plans.

Respect

Respect - it is all good the most wonderful

Respect - you may be beautiful handsome
educated rich or poor but respect is
an open and revolving door

Respect - oh how it is that the world is so
hidden when no one pays attention
to what is seldomly given

Respect - no matter what the weather
no matter what the time may be
no matter what the negative is
no matter what they say

Respect it is the way.

Employment

Money, Money, Money, Money.
Shop till you drop
Employment it is number one to gain
no complain
Employment puts money in our hand
it takes away contraband

Money, Money, Money, Money
Shop till you drop
restaurants, movies, entertainment, vacation
Staycation invest have fun and then some.
It does not matter
but employment gets it and makes it better.
Employment is good
no matter the neighborhood.

Money, Money, Money, Money
Shop till you drop
Employment will be around.
It's up to you to hit the ground.
Employment puts you on the alert
Complain but nothing to obtain
because employment put others to shame.
No matter what take employment
and give it all you've got.

Lonely Heart

Make friends visit family enjoy it all
but the heart is lonely.
Inhale and fill the lungs every breath
makes you feel young.
No one to share or care
that is your misinterpretation
because the heart feels lonely.
Great to believe in everything
watch the river flow the flowers grow
but the action is not sweet
the heart feels lonely.
Never mind the numbness inside,
the laughter the smiles the wide-open eyes
are character of our disguise, the heart feels lonely.

The mountain, the cool breeze
also a part of your fruits and lineage vine.
Let's you see that life is like a tree.
The excitement of it all let you focus
but all in all the heart feels lonely.
Laugh cry, fight, bond, be proactive, pretend it's wonderful.
In everything you feel,
in every emotion you show,
in every exposed gesture,
in every belief you have,
don't use them to close.
what needs repair the most.
The heart feels lonely.

Pets

We are everyone's friend not Just man's best friend.
Guess who we are.
Feed me, play with me, entertain me.
We are not girls and boys.
Rub my tummy throw the toys.
We will get them like girls and boys.
My water fountain, my snack, my fanny pack, my travel bag, my raincoat my shoe where are they,
we are not girls and boys.

Where is my litter, my mouse,
my ball that rolls around the house.
Hey where is my flake
no not cake
my carrot my seed
or even some weeds.
It's me yes me no not the girl or boy.
We run we jump on furniture we walk, we even crawl.
We like to chew on everything.
We hide, we swing like girls and boys laugh it all off we do everything like girls and boys.
Now you know we are everyone's friends.
We are your pets like girls and boys.

Father

Father is loving their children with all they have in,
their mind, soul and heart.
Show emotions to their children to let them know it helps to
express their feelings.
Father is nurturing their children to let them feel wanted.
They let them understand what life has to offer.
Fathers teach their children to develop their own identity.
Teach their children family values,
Father we encourage a bond and let them understand religion.
Father we empower and excite and is the unity to all solutions.

Father we are caring make sure all is ok.
We comfort we show importance, give a smile tell them how to
be a child.
Father yes we know make it simple and easy for them to grow.
Father that we are overcome challenges near and far.
We give you praise. It is hard to let go and watch them grow.
Father we try to groom and see them like flowers bloom as they
grow and prepare to go.
Father hold your head high you also need to be recognized.

Back up Plan

Back up, to the back up, to the back up plan
Don't have one you will fall on your hand
Make it now make it while
you can always have a back up,
to the back up, to the backup plan.

Plan A, Plan B, Plan C.
We do our best to take the first risk
but through it all back up plan is the best.
Back up, to the back up to the back up plan,
figure it out don't lock it in a can.

Remember plans are great but if there is no
back up for your plans they will deflate.

Single Dad

Being Single does not mean we always want to mingle.
Single dad it can be sad.
No one understand that now
we are the mom.
We struggle we try to understand
but single dad
Seldom gets a helping hand.

We try our best we reach out
to let them see we would love to
pass the parenting test.
Single dad we do our best
to raise our children to be prince and princess
Single dad we are proud
to let everyone know
we can stand out in the parenting crowd.

Single dad we will say
parenting has come a long way.
Whatever the circumstance
whatever the challenge
single dad we definitely got it.
Parenting is hard work
because mom and dad
have to be on the alert.
Huray.
Huray best of all
is that single dad can also do it all.

Future

F - Fun, joy, adventure be creative live longer don't give up always see the positive.

U - Uplift, run, jump, hop and skip, socialize Get the most of positive vibe.

T - Tell it all, share your thoughts, grow with the flowers, shine with the sun; stand in the rain to start a fresh day.

U - Unfold let it roll we don't know what tomorrow hold. Enjoy strawberries, plums, apples and pears these will help quench the future atmosphere.

R - Reason, repress, reproach, remember repeat, respect, react the future wants us to know the facts.

E - Endure and make sure to enjoy candy, cakes ice cream, chocolate and every addictive treats. Never underestimate remember the future.
We will embrace and win the future race.

Mother

Mother, Mother you come when I call.
Mother, Mother where are you.
We have taken a fall.
Mother, mother, are you here.
Its quiet outside, are you near.
Mother, Mother do not leave.
Mother, Mother you are our dress,
and we are the sleeves.

Mother, Mother, it's great to know
that you water us and let us grow
Mother, Mother you are always here.
Mother, Mother you are sweet
and make us feel very unique.
Mother, Mother are you prepared
to hear us sing and show we care.

Mother, Mother don't go far
you are the number one.
Our Superstar.

Survival

The bamboo house
The recked boat
gives us the new life
that will keep us afloat
we kiss and hold
hands stroll on the sand
we have survival hand in hand.
The seashell shells sings in our ears
the song that says sugar lips and sexy hips
Survival we will enjoy we don't need
any special toys
Enjoy the natural water the natural food the natural plant on our
Survival Farm

SURVIVAL

The Moon Has A Rainbow

The Color of the arch
and the way the rainbows appears
after a midday shower.
It reveals a smile.
Its arch the way it glows
do we know why its call rainbow.
Let us analyze is it
because it's in the sky.
It shows its face after it feels the rain.
Are the colors reflecting love
or joy also happiness.

The moon the sun and the star
are what we have been told to reach for.
The rainbow is there with an arch
even the upside-down smile.
The moon has shapes but if you look close.
It also has a rainbow.
The vibrant colors that magnify the moon let us see it also have a rainbow.

The moon has a rainbow as vibrant as can be.
It lets you see the circle that embraces it
The moon has a rainbow.
It is elegant inspiring and has great things.
The orange and yellow embrace a mellow mood.
Green and blue excitement is embraced.
Indigo and violet relax and gives off shine like glitter.
Shades of colors mixed together.
The moon has a rainbow it glows in the dark.

Forever

Now is not the time we don't know how
but make it forever.
Mountains may have snow or even rainbows too.
Forever can always tell.
Forever is not a case or an open door
Yes, forever just let us know we can never fade.
Forever is a phrase as well as a phase.
Forever is just another way of saying never.
Think it through forever is not me or you.
Forever is an action that bring reaction.
Let it be known forever is written in stone.

Let It Go

It's best to let it go.
You may get caught up in it.
To lose a nose, an ear, or a toe is not worth it.
Let it go or do you want to keep it.
Is it sentimental just for the hell of it.
Finders keepers or let it go and see the future.
Just because or let it go and take a pause.
Not today it is my way or the high way.
Shucks let it go and loose the ducks.
Better yet let it go and don't feel stuck.

Storm

The hands will always be held high
to protect anything that passes by.
The knees make cracking sounds
but they will hold us up.
We will never hit the ground.
The shady environment may be here
but no storm will tear us down.
Since we will always be prepared.
Thunder storm winter storm
it has nothing to do with weather storm.

Feel right know it by sight storm is always around.
Be sure to tackle them even when they are not around.
Simple storm strong storm
never procrastinate the storm.
Ears are alert to listen for the whispering words.
The storm is brewing getting ready to ruin.
Not today Just you get away.
Our backs are strong our head are definitely on.
So, you see Mr. or Mrs. storm you can't over throw me.

Love Recipe

Shake it, bake it
no matter how you make it.
We need three hundred sixty-six days of love.
Fifteen minutes of kiss.
Forty minutes of holding hands.
The starter kit until you finish the mix.
Put to the side.
I just realize fifteen minutes of cuddle.
Ninety minutes hugs.

Lord, have mercy this recipe contains romance, not just love.
Add half hour of back rub, along with five minutes of foot rub.
Mix ten minutes of massage, and fold in twenty minutes of tickle.
This mixture is getting richer.
Before we bake and put the icing on the cake,
whisk four minutes of whisper.
It will rise to the occasion of folding in.
Twenty minutes of heart beat.
Gentle pour the ingredient of this recipe into you and me.
Let it bake as long as it takes.
Wait before we eat cake,
the final ingredient that is late.
Drop five minutes of smile.
This will definitely make it worldwide.
Let us enjoy this recipe.
It is welcome years round by you and me.

AUTHOR BIO

Deon Marie Llewellyn

Born in Breadnut Hill Ocho Rios St. Ann Jamaica West Indies.

I migrated to the United States November 1980 and lived in Brooklyn then moved to Queens New York.

The Hospitality and Culinary Industry has always been my dream. The love for Writing and Journalizing has supersede that dream.

A graduate from Kingsborough Community College with a Travel and Tourism Associate Degree conferred 1988 has fulfilled my pleasure to travel.

The passion of Culinary Art and the Hospitality industry led me to New York City College of Technology where I achieved a Bachelor of Technology Hospitality Management Degree in 1999. In pursuant of my education, I continued and received a Master's of Business Administration Degree 2010 at Long Island University Brooklyn Campus.

www.ingramcontent.com/pod-product-compliance
Lightning Source LLC
LaVergne TN
LVHW061042070526
838201LV00073B/5149